Awesome Family Activities

*Engaging Activities for Kids Outside and Inside.
Fun Games for any Occasion to Play with a Whole
Family*

By

David Nathan Fuller

All trademarks and brands within this book are for clarifying purposes only and are owned by the owners themselves, not affiliated with this document.

Table of contents

Introduction

It is so important to have family time! You have such a short time with your kids in the grand scheme of things, before they move out and start their own life. This requires us to create lasting memories and strong family bonds which can be created together as a family by doing fun activities at home.

We enjoy doing fun things for the kids that get us out and about, but that's not always possible. One of our top priorities should be finding inexpensive, simple, and fun activities to do at home! If you really start thinking about it, there are so many family activities that you can do together at home. This book will help you discover all of those things you can interact in at home in your family.

Chapter 1: Importance of Family Time

To those who still doubt the importance of family time, a couple of points are mentioned below to put things in a better perspective.

Here are reasons why family time matters:

Creating Closer Links With Your Family

The main reason family time is important is because you need to develop family ties and bonds. Children also want to join gangs or groups to become a member of their society, as they invite them in.

Your children need a sense of belonging and security because they need to feel that they have someone they can turn on and look up to, for anything. Spending family time together means that the family relationship grows profoundly and powerfully.

Owing Time To Talk And Listen

Another good reason to spend time with the family is directly linked to the desire to share, chat, and listen as a family to one another.

Parents also think to talk to their children, who think differently from grown-ups, will be difficult. And parents seem to forget their own day, as when they were young, it was for them! The people you met were mainly those who listened to what you had to say. Likewise, you need to listen to what your children have to say. Listening does not only mean hearing your child's vocabulary but also knowing what your child is trying to communicate.

Without jumping in with questions, questioning, or offering your own opinions, you need to listen. You need to prove you're interested in the discussion, stop all the other research you're doing, and just listen to it. Talk about alcohol and drugs directly to your children, particularly teenagers, and set a good example to yourself.

To Teach Your Kids Important Life Lessons

When you don't teach kids at school, they'll know it somewhere else. As a mom, would you want your kids to learn the essential lessons of life by enduring pain, or going the wrong way?

Although kids need to learn a few things on their own, it's good to have family time for conversations where you can place concerns or problems in front of them, and then speak to your kids about them, ask their advice, and discuss them. It would help them get a better understanding of life circumstances.

To Express Love, Gratitude, And Encouragement

Family time is necessary so that everyone in the family can express love to each other, perhaps by giving hugs, holding hands, being considerate, and loving. Studies show that teens who recall being praised, embraced, or kissed will generally do better at school than those who don't have this experience.

You need to take this quality family time out to ask what each member of the family has done in the day and show interest in the lives of each other. People find criticizing rather than praising very easily. So make an effort to think in each person about the positive and tell your child what kind of goodness you have noticed, besides teaching them these values.

To Instill Family Values Into Your Kids

It is of great importance nowadays to instill family values in children, so that they are not fooled by the number of divorces on the rise.

In the majority of situations, children mimic the actions you display towards them. In the future, if you're an absent parent, they'll be the same with their children. Instead, they sometimes represent worse actions than they see.

So spending family time together will generate a sense of worth and instill healthy family values in your kids.

To Instill Practices And Customs Within The Family

Daily rituals or the little things you do every day and on special occasions help to create within the family a sense of belonging, contentment, and inner comfort. Daily rituals such as how you greet each other or say goodbye to each other, what you do at meals or bedtime, can all be something to share in your family's time.

Families take advantage of being together to celebrate events such as birthdays, anniversaries, or holidays such as Christmas, etc., where they hear about the rituals and what is happening at these times.

To Consider Human Differences

Family time is important if the variations in each family member are to be respected, supported, and valued in the knowledge that each is different in their own way. Let each member of the family be excited about their own personal interests and show respect and tolerance towards them.

Don't pressure members of your family to be like you, or hide their feelings and differences. Enable them to feel proud to be themselves, instead.

Continue To Contact Friends And Relatives

We need to spend time with our family as we live in a society as well as interact with friends and relatives. Knowing that out-of-family people turn to in a crisis can make a difference to the happiness of your child. It also makes them more likely to make good friends later in life.

Sharing The Tasks

Teaching younger children about family time is relevant under your supervision by giving them the chance to do things for themselves. Using adult power wisely, and retain authority with laughter and motivation, not intimidation or threats.

There is a unique relationship between confidence and intimacy by spending time together with the family, which helps to create a healthy family. Especially when kids have a real say in what is going on and where everyone thinks their opinions are being heard.

To Help And To Connect With Your Kids Better

The parental involvement is one of the most overlooked aspects of education today. Most parents don't understand the value of family time and how important it is to get interested in learning about their children.

Every parent and family member has to find the time and make an effort. Research shows that when parents work in the family, their children will:

- For better ratings and test scores.

- High school graduation, at higher levels.

- Are more likely to move to higher education.

- Get positive behaviors and act differently.

Wrap It Up

So, family value and why you should spend quality time with family no longer remain a mystery. You now realize that it helps to build a sense of community where you can share thoughts, ideas, and beliefs.

As a family party, you need to find some opportunities to spend time together and have fun together. You might share meals together, for example, without distracting television or mobile phones, sharing information, and hearing about what happens in each other's lives. You can play cards, games or sports, take vacations together, camp, watch movies or share hobbies.

Through spending more time together, you will create a stronger family bond, and your family will stay together during tough times, in addition to enjoying the enjoyable times together.

Show your family loyalty, stand up for each other so that each person feels secure in support of the family, and come together to form a united front to find solutions.

Kids grow up and are gone before you know it, so don't waste your time with your children and spend it now. Remember, with a positive attitude, shared values, and beliefs that help them cope with challenges, Strong families will put up with losses and crises.

1.1 Why Having Fun with Family is Important?

Your fun skill will be directly related to which category you fall into. "Fun" also means "mess" This is the first fact we need to catch if we're going to have fun. When my friend Cathy splashes with the kids in the puddles, there's sure to be a mess there. Wet, and maybe even dirty, the garments would need to be looked after. It may be in order to showers or pools. This will feel like an obstacle to our day if we don't have the right perspective. However, the right view is that it's an important part of our day. Playing with our kids is part of being a mum. And sometimes, dealing with messes is a part of having fun.

I fall into the category "cleaning." Far too often, the prospect of messes keeps me from having fun with my kids. Over the years, I have come a long way, but in this area, I still have more to learn. I still need to be flexible; at times, I am way too practical. On this one, God collaborated with the mega project that I know my children are happy to do. After my children are gone, I sure don't want to look back and say, "I wish I had loosened up. I wish I would have had more fun. "I want to do it now because I can make the change and make a difference in the lives of my children.

Sparkling Fun

Spontaneous fun often occurs when we optimize the moments. The other day Cathy called, inviting our 10-year-old daughter to her house. Her eight-year-old daughter just had a private yard sale with a couple of relatives. She had her room cleaned out, her things priced and was ready to host this special event. Cathy had been surprised at the business enterprise of her daughter but decided to make the most of the opportunity. She helped Rein set up the sale in the basement on their Ping-Pong table and ordered pizza for the girls who attended this private sale. Opportunities for fun happen regularly – we choose as mothers to either maximize the moments or minimize the fun.

Fun Family

Family fun is a vital part of creating a positive family identity. It creates a bond when families have fun together, that can last a lifetime. Traditions are also formed in fun-filled times. Such rituals allow each family to identify and individualize.

We have a fun tradition at the Savage household called "surprise trips." This began when the older kids were young, and we decided to surprise them with spontaneous activity. In our favorite ice cream parlor, a casual trip to the park, or a matinee showing a new family movie, it could be ice cream. Whatever it is, however, the best part of the fun is anticipation. The excitement increases from the time Mark and I yell, "Surprise Ride," and everyone rushes to get into the car until the time we arrive at our surprise destination. As the children grew older, they also suggested surprise trips. Of course, they aren't really a surprise like that (unless your teen drives Are you somewhere!), but the idea itself says, "Let's have some fun as a family together." It gave us common ground and shared vocabulary that lends family fun.

Holidays also offer enjoyable experiences which can grow into unique traditions. Several years ago, on April Fools' Day, I was serving dinner backward (dessert first!). It was a fun-filled evening that began a new tradition. Since that time, every 1 April has been dubbed "Backwards Day."

Families need to co-create. We need to have unbuilt moments of cohesion. I'm not talking about watching television together-I'm talking about a basketball pick-up game, playing cards, or just sitting on the porch laughing and chatting. Camping, fishing, mountain biking, and hiking are perfect family fun times. We need to take the lead as mothers and make this stuff happen. We have to be available, and we need to appreciate having fun together. We will see our relationships with our family grow stronger as we spend time together in both spontaneous and scheduled events.

Happy Birthday

It's spent the night before birthday planning for a big breakfast. The table is filled with birthday plates, cups, and napkins after the birthday person goes to bed. Presentations of the family are put in the table middle. Later, we slip quietly into their room, hanging balloons and streamers. The room reflects its special day when the birthday girl or boy awakes in the morning. The best part of the party is in as we pass downstairs to the breakfast table: Cake and ice cream for tea! Yeah, I know it flunks all the tests for a nutritious breakfast, but it's the test of time to make fun of the house. It is definitely our family's favorite activity, and with six people in our family, that means we enjoy hot cake and ice-cream six times a year.

1.2 Ways to Bring Your Family Closer Together

There are so many fun activities available for the kids, and we have collected some of them to set you on your way.

1. Museums To Visit

Museum trips are informative and enjoyable and have a knack of sticking in your brain, producing several memorable memories for your young ones. Take a Google search to find out what's on sale, or make a day trip further to plan your travel.

2. Make The Most of A Hot Air Balloon Ride

It is summertime and it is pretty dry. Spectacular sunsets and breathtaking sights can be seen here. You can book a balloon ride at hot air and catch those unique memories.

3. Bake or Cook

Teach your children some kitchen skills, or learn a couple of new tricks yourself. The key thing about cooking is its great fun but also an opportunity to instill some safe tips into the life of your family.

Should not try home-made pizza using organic whole meal flour instead of opting for the more conventional sugary snacks? Throw some wheat germ into the dough mix, mash it and beat it in shape, and then put some in the oven toppings you like: my favorite is asparagus with mushrooms and sweetcorn.

Another special recipe that I can highly recommend is the amazing cauliflower cake from Yutan Ottolenghi. It's something else, and when you bring it up with friends or family, it makes for a nice discussion.

Or, Why not just make some popcorn to keep things simple?

Of course, there's plenty of other recipes to check out. The Green Kitchen app is pretty unassailable for ideas. This one has all kinds of nutritious and ultra-tasty recipes-it comes at a low price, but it's completely worth it for recipes like the immune-boosting turmeric lassie.

4. Go Looking For Treasure

Join with Geocaching, the world's biggest treasure hunt. It's a global event where people are hiding caches and sending you information to go on a treasure hunt. You can search the website to find local ones for yourselves.

5. Start a Channel to YouTube

It's free and easy to do-start a channel on YouTube. You can vlog about everything, or take on something a little bit more ambitious – make a family movie, or chronicle a pet's antics. Don't expect from all this fame and wealth, more of a creative release and a diary of your life.

6. Start Blogging

Should not enter a family forum with an international blogging community? Starting is free, thanks to such services as WordPress. If you love it, you can also pay to upgrade your account-a personal plan is $36 annually.

Why blogging? If you have even the slightest imagination, it can be extremely satisfying to write. It's also a wonderful way to meet new people all over the world online, as well as record what your family has been up to. Looking back down the line a few years makes for great memories.

7. Read More

It's well known how critical it is for children to learn. They will expand their vocabulary through it, and learn more about the world.

But what should I read? Harry Potter is a given, but why not have a session of family reading with something new? I may recommend the illustrated E.H.

1.3 What Makes Family Unique?

You may have noticed that classmates' families at school or among your friends may differ greatly from yours. But the underlying differences are that members of a family prefer to live together. They may disagree or argue, but their love and consideration for each other are closely connected.

Some families have one parent-either, a mother, or a father. Some have both a mother and a father. Others have two moms or two fathers. If two parents' divorce and remarry, you might want to see a double — two sets of parents can be there!

Some kids live in foster parent families who care for them when their biological parents cannot. And there are parents who pursue a legal procedure for adopting or choosing, children they raise as their own.

If adults already have children when they get married, then the marriage joins not only two men but also two families establishing a modern family structure. We name these new families "stepfamilies" — or "mixed" families — as they reflect a new combination of members of the family that were already part of other families.

A parent who is not biologically related to a child considered a "stepparent" (for example, stepmother or stepfather) in a stepfamily. When both parents have prior children, such children become step-brothers and step-sisters to each other.

As many of us know, a family is not limited to just Parents and the biological offspring thereof. The term 'family' is a significant term that includes many other types of loving and guiding relationships.

Family members are also close to each other and believe they can rely on each other for help and support. Whether its grandparents, aunts, and uncles, or even close friends who make up a family, the love or mutual interests that tie them together are what matters.

Regardless of your parental bond, you may be a member of many "families." Your school friend's maybe a family to you. Your soccer team maybe a family.

Chapter 2: Outdoor Family Activities

The outdoors is a perfect place for a family to get together, allowing the weather, how refreshing and energizing the fresh air can be, and encourage friends, parents, and even cousins to bond together!

Fun Family Outdoor events Children:

Let's launch your own home with outdoor activities at the backyard:

Hide and Seek:

Depending on the size of your backyard, hiding and searching is a perfect way for your kids to run and explore while within their own home's protection. The game gets more demanding and exciting as you pair it with your home indoors. If you have even the slightest imagination depending on your children's age so that no one gets lost or hurt during the game.

Backyard Family Fun:

A family home's backyard is an amazing way to have fun with the whole community. Entertainment opportunities are infinite, and anyone will enjoy the grass, trees, nooks, and crannies, and whatever else lies in your backyard. The best thing about backyards is their tons of fun, but they're also really special – some backyards have ponds and rivers running through them, some have 100 + year old trees! As such, here are a few great fun backyard activities to enjoy for the family:

Build a play area with a rock spot. Knew you could make your
own playground for the sandbox? And if you're worried

about bringing little feet of sand into your house, don't worry! We may use dirt, as well. Easy take an area (ideally 5 to 5 feet in width and length) and cordon it off with rocks and stones. Then put to dump gravel within the area (which you can buy in your local shop) within the area between the rocks. Pea gravel is the best gravel to use. Once you've done that, you've built an instant play area that looks like a fun sandbox but avoids all the irritating sand! Another fun addition is to add wooden boards that can be put over some of the border stones if your kid plays with figurines or wheel-containing toys.

Spinning Swing Set:

Others call this the Tarzan swing set, and this common activity for kids takes other professional handicrafts, but it can be done depending on your backyard. To connect two very large trees, it would take a rope, and the rope must be tied on both sides in the form of a very secure knot. You then either need to purchase a spinning swing that can be attached to the rope, or you can create your own by purchasing child-friendly handlebar grips that can be tied to the rope. This activity clearly needs close parental supervision and is more targeted towards children already 12 or 13 years old.

Tree-house Handmade, Similar to the above-mentioned swing operation, this one needs some professional craftsmanship to ensure the health of anyone using it. There is no such thing as you probably already know backyard complete without an awesome tree-house for children to hang out and experience the outdoors. The best treehouse types are those which are waterproof, windproof, and, of course, durable. Since your treehouse needs to be super safe and stable, we suggest that you speak to a builder who can either assist you when you're constructing it or inspect it when it's done so that they can give their professional opinion about its protection.

Outdoor Gardening Events for the Kids:

Gardening: Just like our ideas about indoor gardening above, outdoor gardening is a classic fun family activity where the entire family should come together to unite and enjoy. There are many different approaches to family gardening, and we recommend that you start by taking your children and family to the local gardening store, whether it's a nursery or a plant sale shop.

It's fun to have your children interested in the process early on – they can select seeds, ready-made plants, and other plant equipment they may want to use. Of course, you can occasionally have your kids check in on the plants after you plant the seeds together, make sure there are no weeds nearby, and collaborate on a watering schedule. Before you know it, your kid runs the entire outdoor garden

Places to Go For Family Fun

Taking together: Nothing is more bonding than having a family bike together. When your children is young, it is ideal to start slowly in your local park. Yet once you get off the training wheels, you can start taking local roads, or even quiet streets. Every family is different, but having one parent in the center, the children in the center and the other parent as an anchor in the back makes sense. Also, feel free to partner with another family to make this outdoor community activity even more enjoyable.

Hiking: Not every town has hiking possibilities, but you can certainly check out your local woods (assuming your town has considered it safe). Woods are a perfect place to go on a family walk, where children can explore, dogs can run loose, and parents can enjoy Nature.

Mini Golf: Nothing says more about family fun than a mini-golf outing! Mini-golf tends to be a favorite family for many, as it includes fun and wild golf courses and friendly competition. Only ensure that your kid doesn't strike the ball too hard-he can save it for the range of driving!

Local sports: The fascinating thing about sports games is to watch sports, you don't really need a big sports chain. Each community has its own high school or even college, so there is almost always a football or baseball team to see the locals arrive. This is a great fun family outdoor experience for every family to join.

Ice Skating Rinks: It's a perfect treat to ski with family. What could be more fun than gliding with your children around on the ice, with fun music playing in the background? America is chock with funny rinks, including Miami, Boston, NYC, DC, etc. The best part is, some rinks remain open throughout the year.

Groups Dance

In keeping with the family's theme of indoor activities, maybe consider dance classes for children. There is also no such thing as young for your child to begin to learn how to dance. With dance studios taking on children as young as 18 months, learning to dance early on is definitely a positive activity for your child and can help with the development of both physical and artistic.

2.1 Outdoor Family Activities for Kids and Adults

- **Go fishing**. Learn how to bait your hook and cast your line, and then enjoy sitting together while waiting for a bite.

- **Sell lemonade.** You can not only pass on your favorite recipe for lemonade but also teach some entrepreneurship.

- **Floor a garden.** Why wouldn't we dive in the dirt? Planting a garden will not only give you an afternoon activity, but watering and monitoring the progress of your plant will provide entertainment for months to come.

- **Go to a picnic.** Your grandchildren will help pack up your meal before and after dining and playing in the park. Just keep an eye on our tips for a peaceful picnic!

- **Go swimming**. Visit the nearby pool or lake, and cool off with some water play.

- **Go picking the berry**. You should put your grandchildren to work in the kitchen, baking some tasty berry treats, once you have taken home your haul.

- **Pass the sprinkler in.** Few cries about "summer! "Sounds like kids playing through a sprinkler. Set up a mini water park at the backyard to enjoy your grandchildren.

- **Travel over a kite.** You'll probably have more fun trying to get it into the air than watching it float.

- **Travel to the zoo.** The zoo not only provides a great learning opportunity, but you'll also get your activity to walking between attractions.

- **Catch some fireflies**. Find a jar and punch holes inside the lid, then show your grandchildren how to make "the lantern of nature."

- **Check out the farmer's market.** Take a chance to teach your grandkids about healthy eating and local produce. Buy the ingredients together to shape a great dinner.

- **Go on a journey into Nature.** You could even create a scavenger hunt filled with nature items to be found along the way.

- **Play Frisbee, or catch.** The old American classics never die. Find an old baseball glove, and learn how to throw your grandchildren.

- **Create t-shirts made handmade with tie-dye.** It's a craft you can wear in the summer, and your grandchildren are bound to love making their own version.

- Many children in the generation to come are replacing outdoor play with indoor, sedentary activities such as iPad games, text, or social media. They are much more interested in knowledge-based downtime such as homework and learning than the children of generations past.

How Does Outdoor Play Help Children?

Studies showed children who spent more time outside could be happier and more comfortable. Outdoor time can even improve memory, concentration, and cognitive abilities in the short term. (It's almost like Nature's making us smarter awesome!)

It's up to us to make outdoor play easier

Organize a Playdate outdoors. When your children have friends to play with, it's always more fun, and they're more likely to want to stay outside for longer.

Let your children plot a mini garden. If they are in charge of it, they'll have to go out to the water, weed it and watch it over.

Good, outdoor play is really required. More so now than ever. The more outdoor games that you can promote and enable for your children, the more they will benefit from such play physically and emotionally. A great place to start is creating outdoor experiences for the whole family.

Aid your kids with a rope and an old sheet to build a fort outside. Recommend other things on your fort that would be fun for them to use.

Go for regular walks, bike rides, or family-run. There are trails and bike paths through many urban communities through parks, river ways, or lakefronts.

Lunch with a picnic at the playground or park.

Creates an outdoor scavenger hunt where your kids gather naturally occurring items.

Try to go geocaching. Geocaching is a true game of outdoor treasure hunting with GPS-enabled apps if you've never heard of that. You navigate to a specific collection of GPS coordinates and then seek to locate the secret geocache at that spot. This is a great guide to starting you up.

Make a bucket list of the different parks you would like to try to enjoy.

Go on a hunt for bugs! Give your children a container and have them collect bugs of various kinds.

Turn your yard into a stumbling block. To create fun obstacles, use cones, sticks, a hula hoop, and other items from your garage or backyard.

Seek some new sport: A fun dodge ball, whiffle ball, or football game also a perfect way to help kids love playing outdoors.

Gigantic bubbles blast: Fill a sheet pan with a mixture of bubbles, then dip an over-sized wand to see who can pop the biggest bubble.

Play around with water: Children will jump at the opportunity to go out and sprinkle in the water. There are plenty of imaginative ways to do it: wash the house, water the lawn, run through sprinklers, slip-n-slide down, drop into a blow-up pool, or create a water table.

Eat dinner on the porch, on the deck or in the backyard.

Create Art of Sidewalk: Give a large bucket of sidewalk chalk to your kids and let them go to town. Offer them a few ideas to paint with printed images, or even stencils.

Take 'bouldering' of your children. Children love to climb on things. Take them somewhere that has rocks ready to climb.

Use the strategy for rotation of an outdoor toy. Children are much more excited to play with the toys they haven't seen or can't access in a while. Divide your outdoor toys into three bins and, at the same time, have a big bucket of toys. This may include bubbles, hoops, kites, skateboards, jump ropes, sports equipment, and water squinters.

They had a boat float down a river. Your children are going to be excited to try it out, but you're probably going to have to go on a walk to get to a lake!

Create tasks for your children to do outside, as in the 'Survivor' television series. That's even more fun when there's a reward at the end (one-on-one with Mom or Dad, a night off to help clean the kitchen, etc.)

Make containers for outdoor play. It supports children who are having a tough time thinking about what to do or making choices. Write down various Popsicle stick activities. Let your children choose an activity, and then go outside. Make the things easy to act on – go to the park for 15 minutes, water the plants, set up a water shooting range, pick up a bouquet of dandelions, and draw something with chalk on the sidewalk. So many funny thoughts!

Do your usual everyday tasks outdoors. Do homework, eat food, go baking, read books, or play games outside.

If you're sick of making a mess in your house with your kid's creations, then take them outside! A couple of fun ideas: a play dough picnic, where you let your kids make play dough pretend food. Nature art – gather leaves, flowers, sticks, seeds, and pine cones to produce natural artwork. Outdoor painting – bring an easel and paint to your backyard so that your children can enjoy drawing scenes in Nature.

Stargaze, or look in the clouds for forms. Get a tent, binoculars, or telescope set up and enjoy the night!

Have a bonfire in there, practice good fire-safety habits and oversee all campfire activities. But this is a perfect way of connecting with your mates, making memories, and enjoying the outdoors.

Children can be surprisingly passionate about caring for Mother Nature (and proud of their efforts!) You can make it a game too: a planet-saving mission!

Find a local race to be a member of. If necessary, push a jogging stroller for younger children, and run as a family together.

Ride scooters, motorcycles, tricycles. Build a mini-run, and compete on the wheels.

Have your children pull up weeds? We pay our children one centime per weed, and it definitely gets them out in the yard.

Find a local 'choose your own' and let your kids choose produce from the farm right away.

Play Bug, or Bingo Leaf. Find and identify ten different bugs or leaves.

Nature on the shot. Let our children borrow your phone camera to see how many different wildlife types they can find to take pictures of.

2.2 Outdoor Family Activities in the Backyard

Do you run out of ideas to keep the family busy, to learn, and to have fun? Choose an item from the below list before they realize it!

If you were suddenly surprised to have your kids at home full time, it could be hard to think about new and unique activities to keep them busy while they're out of school. Unfortunately, children get bored quite easily, so having a good list of activities is always an important help.

Or, maybe it is just you and your wife who are planning to spend a lot of time together at the house alone. Staying at home can sound like a blessing, but if you're not used to it, it can also really shake things up. Getting a list of enjoyable backyard events is a great help once again.

So look at these super fun games in the backyard:

1. Lawn Games

Let the games begin at the lawn! They are, however, not just some ordinary games. Those are pretty big games.

Transform your favorite Jenga games into sizes that are more suitable for your wide backyard. This is an easy DIY project have you hanging outside the entire afternoon with your buddies. The children will love this one too.

2. Swing and Gossip

If you've ever been to Mexico's Tulum, you probably fell in love with the bohemian vibes and trendy decor. One element that appears to be everywhere is macramé!

Create your own macramé swings on your patio and enjoy gossiping with your girlfriend on a sunny morning and taking cute pictures.

3. Set up a Hot Bath

A dreamy, twinkle-lit backyard paradise awaits you with a steamy hot tub! Build your own homemade hot tub from a stock tank and allow it to start soaking.

Pour yourself a well-deserved glass of wine under a sky full of stars and steam your troubles away.

4. Twister with Bubble Wrap

A twister game at the backyard might just be the fun you're looking for. A special element is added by covering the mat in bubble wrap. That is making the game even more fun than ever before.

Twister is a wonderful children's game, but did you ever play as an adult? It's the ideal test to see if your yoga classes actually work. Give them a chance!

5. Bar Take

Make your backyard a take bar, and host a luau. It might be a nice way to invest the afternoon with a lot of imagination from your side.

With a happy Hawaiian theme in mind, design and make the food, drink, and decor. Then put some tropical music on and let it work your imagination carry the breeze to a hot sandy beach.

6. Cornwall

A friendly corn whole game is a great way to spend a sunny afternoon with family at your backyard. Or maybe you're like my family, and you'd like to bring in some competition! Does somebody bet?

However, you choose to play on your skin, have fun, laugh, and enjoy the sun.

7. Sketching

Are your backyard birds chirping their delightful songs? Get the notepad and the pencils out and sketch birds of different types.

Do this activity with your kids to teach them the names of the very birds with whom they shared a backyard.

8. Get a Barbecue

Do your cooking for a change outside to get some fresh air. Getting a BBQ is a great way to get around the whole family out for playing, cooking and eating. Make a day out and put out some balloons, party cups, and bring out the board games to the picnic table to play.

9. Domino de law

As we have seen from earlier giant lawn game Jenga, sometimes bigger is better! That's why we love these giant tiles with dominos.

You can make it from scrap wood that you have around the house. We suggest using two ubiquitous boards, but if you have two ubiquitous boards, certainly, it will do the trick.

10. Chalkboard in backyard

Bring backyard fun to fence line all the way up! You can make a good time for any part of your backyard. Build a giant chalkboard on the fence, put in some chalk buckets, and let the imagination run wild.

11. Piñatas

Is there anyone outside who wouldn't like to take their everyday stresses out on a giant papier Mache cocktail just to get candy and gifts in return?

I know I'd have! This giant piñata DIY is so fun and will make for the best pictures from Instagram.

12. Station Smores

Set up in your backyard a Smores station, have a bonfire and make a mess chomping down on some marshmallow goodness.

Make it a special night when you put out take lamps, tell ghost stories, and sip on hot cocoa.

2.3 Outdoor Family Activities in Different Seasons

Outdoor Fun Activities in winter

Most people hole up indoors during the winter months, watching their favorite T.V. shows. The days are dark and short; after all, its cold out, and throwing on several layers of gear just to walk the dog, is no fun.

Wintertime, however, offers an opportunity to experience nature in a whole different way. Outside, there are fewer people and more silence. You can see much of the forest without leaves on the trees. Even during summer months, you can see animals that should have been covered in the foliage.

There are so many benefits of going out in winter. Being active outdoors can help you achieve your goal of calorie cutting and weight loss. It's also an effective way of fighting seasonal affective disorder. The fresh air helps you feel better, and it is much more fun and easier than watching television or browsing the Internet all day long. In short, spending time out in the winter can do a lot of good for you and your family and you will come home in a better mood.

Outdoor Entertainment Gains

Swedes, who live in one of Earth's coldest and darkest environments, spend most of their time outdoors. In their culture, the Nordic concept of friluftsliv (pronounced free-lofts-liv), or "open-air living," is deeply ingrained. As a consequence, they're some of the planet's most fitting and happiest men.

Of course, we would benefit from taking a page from their book. Getting outdoors during the winter months offers physical as well as psychological benefits.

Better Thinking Creatively

If you need some creative ideas, then your best bet is to go for a walk outside.

Research published in psychological journal Studies showed that walking helped 81 percent of study participant's foster innovative thinking, and walking outdoors created more new ideas than walking indoors on a treadmill.

Plus Vitamin D

When you go outside in the sun, you can improve your development of vitamin D. Harvard Health states that in treating anything from heart attacks to cancer to depression, vitamin D can be an important ingredient. We spend 90 percent of our time, unfortunately indoors, according to the Environmental Protection Agency, so we don't get just enough sunlight exposure. And a report published in JAMA found that 2/3 of adults and teens in the U.S. are vitamin D deficient.

The good news is that having your regular dose doesn't take a lot of sun exposure-10 to 15 minutes will do the trick.

Positive effects on health

Work is seen in the journal Nature that individuals who spent at least 30 minutes a week in a green area, such as a park, had lower blood pressure and depression levels. The report also cites a further 17 research projects that have linked outdoor time to positive effects on health, including:

- Shrinking stress
- Few allergies

- More social wellbeing

Lower cardiovascular mortality

Outdoor spending time also helps to prevent nature-deficit disorder, especially among children. The disorder of design deficiency is not a medical condition. The nature-deficit disorder can lead to multiple physical and mental illnesses, including diminished sensory use, higher rates of physical and emotional illness, attention difficulties, higher rates of near sightedness, and obesity in children and adults.

Healing Skills

Spending time outdoors could potentially improve the healing process for your body.

A thesis report by the University of Pittsburgh published in the journal Psychosomatic Medication found that patients undergoing spinal surgery and staying in the sunniest unit of the hospital experienced less pain and stress and needed 22 percent less medication per hour than patients in darker units.

Prepare the Cold

Swedish parents have a saying to their children that they sometimes repeat: "There is no such thing as bad weather, just bad clothes."

The cold-weather gear is a must if you want to enjoy yourself. Don't just go out under your coat in boots, jeans, and a jumper! Layers are important. Wear thermal leggings under your jumper, and many layers of moisture-wicking: cover gloves and a hat.

If you're not cold and hot, then after five minutes, you're more likely to enjoy yourself and not run back inside. Investing in quality outdoor clothing, as you'll get with brands like Patagonia, makes winter activities definitely more enjoyable.

If you have children, always make sure they are dressed appropriately. Younger kids are more likely to run outside with only a T-shirt under their coat. Often pack a full change of clothes for each child as well as plenty of snacks and drinks when you go out.

Fun Ideas in winter

For many people, it's hard to get ready to go out during the winter. Our normal inclination is to hibernate and snuggle before March rolls around.

And how can you get out there yourself? Small start. Tell yourself that you are going to just go out for 15 minutes. This is it. And once the 15 minutes' time is up, you can get back inside.

It works for many people because it is not much of an engagement. You don't think of going on a day-long snowshoeing excursion-you're going out for 15 minutes. Anybody can do it.

And when you get outside and start moving around, you start warming up. The cold air keeps your system vigorous, and you feel good. The first 15 minutes until you know it can easily turn into 30 minutes.

Gliding around a frozen pond or ice-skating rink is always pleasant. Unless you own a pair of ice skates, first check out thrift stores, as you can usually find a couple for a few dollars. Used skates can also be found on eBay.

Go astray

A Swedish fitness craze, blogging is gripping the whole world now. "Plogging" is a two-word combination, "plocka," meaning "pick" and "jogging." Blogging is a part of the workout and part of social responsibility.

You go jogging while blogging, and at the same time, pick up litter. The Washington Post notes that blogging is actually better than jogging because you integrate squats and bends into your run, and blogger's burn an average of 50 calories more than normal joggers per 30-minute workout.

And that's not anything you need to continue doing. Cold-weather running gear is a must, such as thermal running tights and a moisture-wicking beanie. You must also bring with your plastic or latex gloves to pick up trash and a trash bag to carry it in.

Painting in the Snow

Snow painting is an entertaining outdoor activity for children who bounce off the walls after they are stuck indoors. There are a couple of items you must have on hand:

- Food coloring in the key three colors: red, blue and yellow
- Each child has a small spray bottle or small bowls and paintbrushes
- Fill each bottle with water to create "spray paint" and add a few drops of food coloring until you have reached the perfect color range. If your child prefers to paint with a brush, mix the coloring in a bowl with the food and water.

You can make several other colors using the three primary colors. Many food coloring boxes have instructions for making different colors, or these variations can be used:

Yellow + blue = verdant

Red + Blue = Lilac

Red + orange = yellow

Encourage your children to build a snowman or snow fort, and then use the paint to decorate them.

Go fishing on glace

If your family has a good time fishing during the warmer months, when the weather turns cold, there's no need to pause. Ice fishing is an exciting and unique way to go fishing. But if you are not careful, then this can happen; be careful, be risky. If the ice isn't thick enough, you may fall through, which can quickly turn fatal if you aren't rescued right away.

Most bait shops and fishing stores remain conscious of the local conditions. To be safe, however, never fish on ice, which is less than 4 inches thick. And avoid rivers, since the forming of thick ice is harder for moving water. The lakes and wetlands are healthier. Popular Mechanics has an informative article about ice fishing and the do's and don'ts and what you need to start.

Shoveling snow for the poor

Snow-shoveling is a perfect outdoor exercise, and every 30 minutes, you can burn about 223 calories. Through shoveling snow for someone in your neighborhood or group, such as a local senior or a relative who's sick, you will reinforce the good feelings of this activity.

Take Pictures

To some people, winter seems bleak and gloomy, particularly when compared to summer's bright and colorful bounty. But, if you stop and look, the sparseness and clean winter lines have their own beauty.

Take your camera out into the woods and take winter landscape photos. Look out for tiny information as you walk, like a pine cone partly covered in snow or a branch of bright-red hawthorn berries that the birds have not yet noticed. Listen to the crunch of your feet bobbing on the snow or the chitter of chickadees on the branches above.

The outdoors in the winter months are full of life and beauty, giving you the opportunity to take some beautiful photographs. Everything you need to do is walk out and look.

Head to campsite

Yes, you read that correctly. In the winter, people go camping. When snow is on the ground, it's called "snow camping." And if you have the right gear, it can be an exciting and unforgettable experience.

There are several reasons you should try camping in the snow. First, there is a good chance that you are going to be the only one out there. It's just you, your family, and the beautiful forests, and for a great campsite, you don't have to think about battling the crowds. There's no mosquitoes, ticks, poison ivy, or rain, either.

When you've set up your campsite, there's plenty of ways to enjoy the wild.

- Go tubing in the snow

- Stargaze – stars are even more apparent in winter due to the clear atmosphere

- Create a bonfire and samaras

- Go rollerblade

- Explore the woods while hiking in winter

- Identify tracks on animals in the snow

- Winter camping has its drawbacks, and it's an activity that needs unique and often expensive equipment.

- Cold-weather apparel, cold-weather sleeping bags rated at least 10 degrees below the lowest temperature you'd expect to experience, sleeping pads, and a four-season tent are all necessary.

Go Mountaineering

Snowshoeing is an exciting experience that everyone in your family should seek. It's not a big investment when you have to buy clothing. Often, the price of a nice pair of snowshoes is less than what you would pay for two days of skiing. And snowshoes, if you take care of them, last a long time.

Go on a Hunt for Treasure

Food coloring is the best friend of a parent, and this magical ingredient can be used to create frozen "gems" for your children to find.

They are using water to fill an ice cube tray, placed in a few drops of coloring food in each mold, and pop the tray into the freezer. When the water freezes, ice cubes are formed, which look like gems, hide those gems around the yard, and let your children go hunting for treasure.

Move behind the yard

There will be days when you literally do not want to leave home. Luckily there are plenty of outdoor artistic things you can do right in your backyard.

Create angels out of snow.

If the temperature is below 32°C then go out and blow bubbles on the wand, which freeze.

Bring your cookie cutters outside and let them make "snow cookies" for your babies.

Make snow-sculptures for animals

String up popcorn or cereal using a needle and thread, and decorate a tree that you can see from a window within the home. For days, you will hear birds and another wildlife nibble happily over it.

Hollow an orange out and fill the husk with birdseed to make a feeder for a bird.

Start a snowball fight.

Create maple syrup taffy out of snow-see the directions in the kitchen's post.

We are using sticks in the snow to allow the draw.

Create snow lanterns using the Little Green Fingers tutorial.

Grab your beach toys and let your children make moats and snow castles.

Outdoor Fun Activities in summers

Parents face the challenge of keeping kids happy during the long summer break. You need to plan ahead to shorten the times you hear, "I'm bored." Check out these 60 outdoor activities and pick those that will keep your kids happy for the whole summer.

Games in Practice

Balloon Volleyball-Set up your court to divide your yard into two by using a jump rope (or any rope). Using a ball basket, and provide alternative serves for matches. The winner is the first to 21!

Blanket Relay-Take some blankets (preferably old ones) and pull your partner over the lawn as quickly as possible. Group leaders swap positions to have a ride to the finish line for their friend.

Mini-Golf Course-Probably your garage has everything you need for this game — pool noodles, ropes, and boxes of cardboard. Arrange all to build your very own course on your driveway or yard.

Driveway Toy Car Race-Pick up any sort of toy car and a few sidewalk chalks sticks. Draw in the driveway the start and end lines and the lane markers, and let the races start.

Frisbee Tic Tac Toe-A cheap shower curtain, colored tape, and nine Frisbees are required. Tap the curtain of the shower to the ground, and make a Tic-Tac-Toe grid with the tape. Stand to throw a Frisbee on a square behind a given line. Enable the players to land multiple attempts in a square.

Glow in the Dark Bowling-Pop glow sticks in 10 water bottles to make bowling pins that you can use at night.

Lawn Twister-For outdoor fun using circular stencils and paint the game board onto your lawn.

Outdoor Field Hockey-To create a DIY version of field hockey, catch pool noodles, balloons, and a laundry basket. Score a target in your laundry basket, use the pool noodles as the stick to push the balloon around your lawn.

Paper Boat Race-Make paper boats and race them in a kiddie pool to propel them by blowing them through a straw.

Obstacle Course-To create a backyard course, use objects you already own, such as jump ropes, boxes, and hula-hoops. It will thrill your children and put their talents to the test. Encourage your children, with their own ideas, to change direction.

Shaving Cream War-Stock up on cream to shave. Shake can spray opponents from the neck down for 20 seconds, then an adult says, "Go." Hose off by the time the game is over.

Watermelon Seed Spitting Contest-Liven up with some friendly competition an afternoon. Challenging the children to see who can better target or spit the farthest.

Projects in Sculpture

Body Painting-Let the children paint themselves and each other with washable tempera paint, then let the sprinklers wash it away. It is recommended that you use old swimsuit or clothes.

Flower Painting-Dip the whole flower into the paint and use it to make original artwork as a paintbrush.

Fly Swatter Painting-The the use of a fly swatter is a big twist to art creation. Selecting one that has a unique pattern will encourage your child to whip up a unique masterpiece.

Journal of Photography-Inspire your children to take photos to document their day. It's an interesting way to look through images to a day in their lives.

Sun Melted Crayons-Pick all those crayons are broken together with aluminium foil, cookie cutters, and a paper plate. Place the foil then top with the cookie cutters on a paper plate. Remove crayons broken, and through them in a sunny spot. The newly formed crayons pop out of the cookie cutters once they have melted. Put the new crayons to use then.

Art Sale-Make good use of those skills by planning an opportunity to give back. Build a stand and have kids in the neighborhood take shifts selling unique artistic creations, from pottery to crayon drawings. The money raised can go to a charity favorite.

Rucker our Nature

Create a Birdhouse-Transform Popsicle stick into a birdhouse. Paint the chickens, and hang them.

Camp Out at Your Backyard-With the comforts of home close by, your family can enjoy the great outdoors. Build a roasting fire for hot dogs, and melt marshmallows for s' mores.

Design a Fairy House-Gather branches, leaves, and flowers, and then add a ton of imagination to create a house for the fairy.

Favorite Park-Get your nearest parking map. Visit them all and vote for your choice.

Glow in the Dark-Capture fireflies in a jar at night to see those curious insects. Release them at the end of the evening back into Nature.

Bug Hunt-Take a clipboard, a piece of paper, and then head outside. It could be fun to have a magnifying glass and plastic jar too. Encourage the children to list or draw any bug they see. Come count all the ants you find for an added twist.

Stargazing-Learn about the constellations and have a few star maps printed out. You can spread a blanket one night, and look for these recognizable star groups.

Mud Pies-Let the children get muddy while having a lot of fun. Then pour water and mud into buckets and turn over to make mud pies. Decorate with seeds, twigs, and leaves.

Nature Walk-Go for a stroll, and collect Mother Nature objects. Back at home, make a collage from items found.

Plant a Garden-A garden is a great way to teach children how to grow their own meals. A garden should keep them busy all summer between watering and weeding, and you get to eat the harvest.

Picnic in a park-Take the children to a state or national park and show them how vital it is to protect beautiful property. Take along a diary or sketch pad to document the experience.

Farmer's Market Visit-It's a great opportunity to sneak into a little nutrition education and get them more interested in what they're eating. Let your kids try and pick something new.

Fun in the Community

Bike Parade-Reach out with children to your neighbors for a parade in the neighborhood. Encourage participants to decorate their ride with flags, streamers, and balloons. Let them play as parents cheer them on together.

Ice Cream Truck Hunt-Let the truck go a little ahead of your house and track it down for a tasty treat. Your kids will be on their neighborhood block for an adventure.

Community Bike Wash - Take a bucket, a sponge, and a hose to set up a neighborhood kids' bike wash and raise money for a local charity.

Neighborhood Game Night-By playing kickball, soccer, and capturing the flag, organize a multifamily competition. Team up fathers and daughters vs. sons and mothers. Designate another parent to be a referee.

Move Night-There's no need to go to a local park to create an outdoor film experience. Rent a projector, set up in a community yard or open place, spread out the covers and enjoy some popcorn.

Skills

Cardboard Fort or Castle-Walk into your nearest supermarket or appliance store and bring a bunch of boxes back with you. Consider yourself a part of the building crew, since you are likely to be the person responsible for cutting with a craft knife. Your children should tape it up and paint the structure.

Rock Art-Find and paint rocks for use as garden ornamentation, paperweights, or pet rocks.

Seashell Art-Your kids can paint, string, or glue them together. Only a few supplies and a creative mind are the only things needed

Totem Poles-Make totem poles out of paper towel rolls. Spread out an old cloth as a base camp on your porch or patio to construct and paint this art project.

Challenges in mind

Map It Out-Show some examples of maps to your kids. To build their very own map, make them think about their neighborhood. Take a walk or drive once drawn, to see if you can follow along.

Neighborhood Scavenger Hunt-This fun game blends a scavenger hunt with a neighborhood walk. Write down 10 to 15 things you should look for in the neighborhood stroll, including street signs, garden decorations, different plants, birds, and animals before you leave home. The winner is the first person to come across a single item.

Ball Park Time-Go to a local baseball game to help your children learn how to maintain a scorecard.

Plan a Treasure Hunt-Send your kids on a treasure hunt with a bit of advanced planning. Start with a homemade map that you stained with coffee, and the edges were scorched. At the end of their adventure, get some prizes.

Take a Heads or Tails Road Trip-Flip a coin each time you hit an intersection to see Playing in the bath.

Aqua Limbo-For a limbo game using the stream from a water hose as the ring.

Balloon Babies-Fill up a balloon with water and draw a face on it. Wrap your child in a towel and give her a new baby. For how long a balloon splits before she can take care of it.

Tricycle Car Wash - You can turn your driveway into a tricycle riders' car wash with a package of PVC pipes and a garden hose. Swimsuits are required to splash this good time

Homemade Sprinkler-Take a bottle of 2 liters soda and poke holes in it. Connect a male-to-male adaptor to a hose in the yard. Let them hang or throw over a branch of a tree. Change the flow of the sprinkler by changing the flux of water.

Water War-Crank up the hose, fill the arms and balloons with water, and turn on the sprinkler for a water war. This is a good activity on a hot day and a fantastic substitute for a pool.

They are creating Ice Block-Fill different containers with a mixture of water and food coloring. Take them back, until frozen. Pop the molds out and let the children build towers, trains, and buildings before all melt.

Ice Painting-Colored ice paint. Just freeze ice cube trays on washable tempera paint. It is a fun way to cool off your kids, create art, and get messy.

Slip 'n Slide-Buy colorful plastic sheeting and secure downhill on a slight slope with the hose water running. To raise the fun factor, add swimming pool floats.

Sponge Bull's Eye-Paint the eye of a bull on the street, and add a point value to every target circle. Children stand at the start line, throwing a wet sponge at the target.

Squeeze the Sponge Relay-for each of your babies, and you will need two buckets-one filled with water and one empty. Give one sponge to each of the babies. The purpose of the game is to use the sponge to move the water from bucket to bucket. The winner is whosoever does it the fastest.

Squirt Gun Painting-Apply color, instead of putting water into a squirt gun. Children will squirt the paint onto a paper sheet to make art in a fun way.

Take a Refreshing Stroll-Wade through a creek searching for tadpoles or minnows. For a catch and release, take your net along.

Unfreeze Your Reward-Put small toys in an ice cube tray like plastic bugs, bikes, or dolls. Add water and allow it to freeze. Pass every child a cube over. Let them melt before prizes appear while holding them in their pockets.

Water Balloon Dodge Ball-Using water-filled balloons as a dodge ball. Play, as usual, just remember that you don't hit the faces of men.

Water Balloon Piñata-Fill, the balloons with water, tie them and string them between two trees or along a line of fabric. Let children take turns smashing the balloons with a stick without all the sugar for a fun summer twist.

Wet Sponge Tag-The, The first person, tags another person, starting with a soaked sponge, tossing the sponge onto a different player to give them "It." Note, don't aim for the nose! Whether you are going right (heads) or left (tails).

Outdoor Fun Activities in the rainy season

Children love running in sprinklers and splashing in fountains, so why not take advantage of it when water falls down from the sky? Such ideas for rainy day outdoor activities will get you going, but it's your creativity that limits you. Unless a thunderstorm is out! That case just stays inside and wait for a lightning-free rainy day. You can then go out and enjoy the raindrops that fall on your head, the puddles to splash in, and more.

Outdoor rainy-day activities-children in raincoats

Equip yourself with old clothes, raincoats, and boots (or water shoes if it's warm-up) and show those boss puddles. Daily rainy-day walks around your city, or Favorite Park will help you find the spots that usually form the biggest, most splashy puddles.

Color racing

Make your own rainbow: Take the chalk outdoors during or after a rain. For an effect that is very different from dry-land chalking, the moisture intensifies and blurs colors.

Sprinkle with a few drops of coloring food or tempera paint powder onto a sheet of paper (or other durable pieces of paper) for more colorful rainy fun. Take it out, and let the rain give you aquarelles. To make designs, you can swirl the liquid around. Bring the plate to dry inside, or press another piece of paper on top, then peel it off to make a printout.

Dress up children in swimsuits or old clothes on a dry, summer-rainy day, then send them out with washable or bath paint. They should, in no time, have purple wings, green arms and hands with polka dots.

Float Your Plane

You can float and see how tiny boats (or twigs and leaves) toy fly if your yard or park offers up puddles and trickles of moving water. Challenge the children to build dams from artifacts found. If you cannot find a good puddle, use a large rimmed baking sheet or plastic tub to build your own.

Drip, Press, fall

Stash a cheap or disposable waterproof camera away for rainy days. You can then take a walk and let the children snap away. They can think big and catch rain clouds or large puddles, or zero in on raindrops that are posed delicately on a leaf or spider web.

Create Pies in Mud

Dirt, did he? You will have mud than on a rainy day! For a mud-pie bake-off, take old aluminium pastry plates and other plastic containers outside. Adorned with leaves, sticks, rocks, and even small (sturdy) toys or pieces of household recyclable materials. Also, don't forget to place them in the recycling bin when you have your pies baked.

Building a World

Does your child have plastic creatures, dinosaurs, or other tiny figurines? Bring them out into the rain to discover the puddles, the water, the piles of leaves, and more creations of Nature.

You can break out bath toys or other water toys for rainy-day games, too. When done, clean them with moist, soapy water (or better yet, let the kids do it).

Drop the Rain

Get scientific, and make a rain gage to calculate how much rain you actually get. Place it outside, and periodically check it to see. You may even want to keep a log (this also makes for a great science fair project).

Make Fine Music

Let children help you find household objects that can make music: pots, pans, spoons, plastic containers, and pieces of cardboard if they want to play. Bring them outside to listen to how it sounds like raindrops dropping onto different surfaces. Children may also want to try stirring water inside a bucket or bowl or pouring it from one container into or over another.

Catch fish and franks

When you have access to a pond, stream, or lake, rainy days are perfect for fishing and frog-catch. You can float tiny toy boats (or twigs and leaves) and see how they travel, for stranded earthworms keep an eye out. Most children love to "rescue" a worm from the pavement gently, and return it to the grass or dirt.

Chapter 3: Indoor Family Activities

Home Indoor Games for Children

There are several reasons for having your family keep things indoors. If it's the heat, the cold, or any other excuse you might think about having a roof over your head, well, that's totally true.

And the truth is, there's no reason you need to have fun with the family indoors. Family activities, including your living room, den, and even your kitchen, can be held anywhere!

The list is really, really, never-ending in terms of indoor events that the entire family will enjoy.

Pleasant Card Games for Family

Apples to Apples: If your family still has Apples to Apples to play together, it's time to get on with the program! This incredibly famous game has also won awards (Games Magazine's Party Game of the Year in 1999) and is a total blast for even friends to play with family members. To any player, the way to play the game is to play their Red Apple cards, each of which has a noun, to try and win the most rounds. In answer to the Green Apple card shown by one player for all to see, these cards are played and read aloud, and the card includes an adjective or a summary. The successful player selects their favorite Green Apple card, and the winner is whoever selects the coin!

Can you think this classic card game, which entertained families in their living rooms, was invented only in 1971? Uno is a family play game that is highly enjoyable and perfect for all ages. Parents and children alike will enjoy playing it. We presume you know how to play this amazing family game, but we'll leave it to the original developers to clarify the rules of this family-friendly card game if you don't.

Family-Friendly Board Games:

Monopoly: This is a classic family board game that can be a fun yet time-consuming activity for teenagers, siblings, parents, and grandparents! We'll spare you the specifics of how to play this game because every family knows how to play this game on the board.

If you're a family that's super competitive, then you probably want to win when you play. We find a very excellent guide on how to win a game of Monopoly on that notion, with some great advice here. Warning: if you dominate your siblings/kids, your family may get annoyed!

Trivial Pursuit: This game is more suited for families with older siblings, who have a little more international experience and can answer simple trivia questions. When you have an adolescent in your house, then Trivial Pursuit is a fun family game that everyone will enjoy.

Trivial Pursuit is an immensely successful board game, with over 100 million copies sold and appearing in 17 different languages in over 26 countries!

Activities Indoor Planting:

Planting is an art overlooked in one's home, school, or workplace for things to do. That is because, even for the outdoors, people still presume both planting and gardening. That's certainly not the case, and you can definitely do a lot of fun planting events with the whole family.

Venus flytrap: Let's continue with the easiest and a favorite of fans as well. We are definitely no experts here at UNICEF Kid Power when it comes to plants, and here is a great tool for official information on this product.

The best thing about Venus Fly Traps is they really can be grown indoors. It is essential, however, that you position the plant by a window, ideally one which is opened regularly. The open window can be in every part of the house, but it must touch the plant by the sunlight. Clearly, the fun part is feeding on the plant.

Whether your kid has patience, he might get to see the Venus flytrap catch a bug such as a fly or a bee. Nevertheless, if you feed your Venus flytrap into different treats, like tiny pieces of chicken or fruit, it is certainly a fun thing to do. Make sure your kid doesn't feed it with anything ridiculous like a crayon or clay-it can kill the plant!

Plant racing: We'll have to explain what we mean by racing here before you get too excited. Essentially, this would be a competition between family members, on whose plant it can grow the fastest. It would make sense that a bit of friendly rivalry would be the best way to stoke curiosity from all family members.

Essentially, each member of the family will get its own identical seeds, soil, and flower. Everyone is on his own after that! Every single person responsible for their respective plants is responsible for watering it properly, give it the right amount of sunlight and maybe be creative with other plant-growing creative ideas (it comes to mind playing Mozart near the plant). The plants can be carried close to one another every week, and weighed to see who has grown the most! Other factors such as first seeds to sprout may also be calculated, and variations in leaf structure, color, or consistency.

Family Gymnastics activities:

Gyms are ideal for poor weather and rainy days. Whether you need a running outlet for your kids or an intramural basketball pickup league, there's something you can do. Now, if you can rent a part of the gym for your family to enjoy, the sky is the limit to numerous fun family activities related to gymnastics, and here are our favorites:

Octopus Dodge Ball: This game includes the traditional dodge ball rules, but the player only sits in the place they were hit instead of heading off to the side after being hit by a ball. Then these sitting players can tag anyone running by them, forcing them to sit down, too. You are going to have an octopus-shaped with family members soon enough!

Spin and Run: This is an essential race, probably best between only two members of the family. Why maybe ask? Okay, to have so many dizzy people running around isn't a smart idea. The basic premise is to have two men, preferably siblings, each taking a bat or a ball and keeping it over their heads, looking at the bottom of it and then spinning around ten times. THEN these two dizzy siblings sprint to the finish line with each other! And yes, the result is hilarity.

Hula Hoop Freeze: Get a few kids with hula hoops spinning around. They can make only hula hoop until the count is up to 10. Then, anyone can tag them, and then they're IT. Of course, someone who uses the hula hoop is invisible from someone else's being frozen.

3.1 Indoor Activities for Family and Kids

Tinker toys with Marshmallow

Everything you need to create the perfect puffy is a bag full of marshmallows with some thin pretzel sticks. Your child just skews the sticks with the marshmallows to make his own masterpiece. Connect to the fun by bringing in the house toys (dog, teddy bear) or other animals and challenge them to be big (bad wolf) and to blow or smash it down, your brother.

Cookie-Sugar Pizzas

Even the chef challenged most domestically can pull off this sweet and easy project. Slice a roll of (refrigerated) sugar cookie dough into several thick cookies. Mildly flatten them on a cookie sheet for about 10 minutes to spread, bake it, and cool off. You can then decorate your little Dominique Ansell's With red sauce topping or raspberry jam, shredded cheese coconut.

Bingo Family-Photo

Develop the memory of your boy, and help him learn who is with this picture game in your family tree. Take nine family pictures and group them into 3 rows, then give your child 9 pieces of play cards or checkers to serve as chips for bingo. If someone calls Grandma or Daddy or the picture is replaced with the card by your Toddler. Whoever gets three wins in a row will have game win.

Greetings to Grandparents

Haul out supplies for the craft and set up a Hallmark home company. First, your kid designs the card with pictures of stickers, glitter, cut-out magazine, or something else he wants. Then you ask the receiver what he needs to say, and you write it inside. (I once got one of those from my then 2-year-old nephew who said, "Dear Tante Isadora, I want to bite my piggy toy. Love, Jared." That's one of the cards I've never tossed.) The cake icing? Let's your child seal the envelope and slip it into a nearby mailbox when the weather is clearing.

Build a Sensory Table

Recall the slimy pleasure of screwing your hands at the local haunted house through a basket of replacement eyeballs (aka peeled grapes)? Except for the hallucinations, this practice provides similar thrills. Fill a set of bowls or washbasins full of textured objects. Peeled grapes are still a good choice, as are steel-wool sheets, cold cooked spaghetti, dry beans or corn-starch. Blindfold your boy, screw his hands through him and explain what he feels like. Challenging him then to guess the object.

Signature Narration

This is a tactic that I use at bedtime to give old stories a new start. Start reading and narrating one of the favorite books your child likes. When you reach a crucial point in the story, ask him to take credit for the tale and add his own twist. Like, if you're reading book on Cinderella and she's torn up her dress by the mean stepsisters, ask your kid, "What would you do if anyone did that to you? Would Cinderella just run away and cry, or should she do something else that help?"

Bowling-a-Rama

Thin, an empty (water) bottles, and a rubber ball all you need to turn the family room into a bowling alley — without, of course, stupid shoes. Six bottles should be enough for bowling pins; fill them with a dry pasta for or little water with some extra weight if the bottles fall over too easily.

The group at Barbie Beach

Grab a set of Barbies bikini-clads, beach towels (washcloths), sunscreen (baby lotion), and maybe one or two yachts (some Tupperware), and head for some fun in the pool. Hint: most Barbie's are really loving their diving board (faucet). The opinion of my daughter: Sunglasses and a tropical drink (iced juice in a Sippy cup) make the feeling equal to a holiday in St Tropez.

Down the Disco

Disco has been dead and revived so many times, I'm not sure whether it's either inside or outside. But I do know that young children love to dance to it, even though they think "Bee Gees" is some sort of a snack that you refuse them. Dim the lights, close the blinds, hand over a flashlight to each child (for Total disco effect), and a tiny scarf was twirling around.

Cinema Season

Even the most imaginative parent will have to return to some nice, old TV time at some point. Keep a secret stash of DVDs that you only take out when the weather is cruddy, so rainy-day television is a treat. The same old story about Wiggles is somehow boring for that child whose play opportunities are minimal.

Pirate Cheers

Somehow, Caribbean fever pirates have tricked their way down to the kid's package. Doing something even remotely like a pirate sends me into happiness paroxysms, so try this treasure hunt. Wrap a bunch of aluminium foil wooden blocks and hide them around the house (don't get too clever — remember with whom you're dealing). Give each child a tiny paper bag and a flashlight, and challenge them to find the hidden silver.

Mini Car Washing

Gather the fleet of cars, trucks, and spaceships from your child for a thorough job that will embarrass your local garage. Load all of them into the tank, and give them plant spray cleaning and empty squeeze bottles.

Tape-Masking Marvels

Who would have thought too much of it fun a modest roll of masking tape would provide? Give the living room floor a hopscotch pattern or mock balance beam. Or have tapes with markers in your child's color, and use them to "template" his own T-shirt. My personal favorite: The dollhouse invisible. Lay down on the rug a "floor plan" and fill the house with doll furnishings.

Get it together!

I had contemplated building a doghouse for a long time Internet-bought plans. I was in my workshop waiting for the timber. I had interested my son in the project when a bad-weather day came and ripped the box open. Within about three hours, we designed a doghouse.

Picnic at the family-room

Adjust staff by serving meals outside the cooking. First, seize your basket (you don't need a basket picnic basket a laundry basket is going to do it) and put together some picnic foods the kids can "pack" themselves — juice boxes, paper plates, water bottles, napkins, string cheese, raisin packets etc. While the kids are busy filling the tub, spread a blanket over the family room, and put some sandwiches together.

Cosy family time

Our 15-month-old son usually keeps himself busy on a rainy day by getting us loads of books to read to him. We also have two big dogs in the house that go stir-crazy and give him hours of entertainment!

3.2 Indoor Fun Activities on Rainy Days

Day (or Night) for Family Movie

What is something better than cuddling up a blanket and a cup coffee with full of snacks for a family plus movie night with your kids? Not too many. My children enjoy the luxury of chowing at munchies and watching a movie.

Transform your family room or den into personal theater, on the next rainy day or night. Find a good movie that will please the entire family and enjoy the film!

Bed Blanket

All toys are great when there's a blanket fort inside, believe me. Help your children build their super-fort in the household room when the next rainy day comes around.

My boys are going to keep busy drawing or playing with their action figures for hours since boring old toys take on a new life when they are under cover of a blanket for some reason.

Playing Day for Family

If you prefer to spend time with your family without a computer, try a classic board game. Board games are a great way to invest your free time leisurely day at home, whether you're buying up real estate in Monopoly game or avoiding the enticing sweets in Candy Land. Build a Tent with Blanket.

Build a Stick for Rain

Gather a tinfoil, masking tape, paper towel tube, dry rice, crayons, and a long pipe cleaner if you are feeling crafty. Decorate the entire paper towel tube and make your child paint on it. First, fasten your tinfoil with masking tape to one end. Coil and fit the pipe cleaner into the container, along with the rice. Secure tape and tinfoil to the other end of the tube. The rain stick for your child is now able to make calming sounds of rain!

Cook for each other

Spend the day all together doing a shooting family-favorite meal so long as the kids are trapped indoors? Allow cooking fun with your chiefs (assistant) by assigning them tasks. My youngest likes to blend with spices and herbs, while my eldest likes to shake.

They'll not only feel valuable and useful, but they'll also be proud that they helped make it. Plus, you get the week to do some cooking.

Hunting doggy Scavenger

Include him in your rainy-day adventures if you happen to have a furry (Dog) friend inside your family. Hide dog's treats in the puppy-friendly locations, and see if your dog can find all the secret prizes out. Track his success and see if, on the next rainy-day, he can beat his record.

Play Seek and Hide

Yeah, I know its kind of a simple one, but little kids love it simple. Using the house as a whole and get imaginative with the game rules. For example, children must recite the alphabet rather than count it to ten.

The children aren't going to be too hard to find. Typically mine pops out of their hiding places as soon as I walk in. (Play it up a little bit and say they can't find it.

Have a Party for Dance?

Aid release with some loud music some of their almost limitless strength. Dancing around the house can help you work off pent-up energy and get some exercise.

Read a Right Book

Cuddle up your children with their favorite book in a blanket and read it together — or start a series together like Narnia's Chronicles or Harry Potter. Take turns on reading, or make them read to you to keep them focused and interested.

3.3 Indoor Fun Activities in Summers

Owing to the hot weather during the summertime, it's not a safe idea for children to play outside all day long. There are really so many activities your kids might do indoors. They can experiment with a craft, learn cooking skills, or play some fun games that are educational. Additionally, enjoyable indoor activities can create special memories.

Boats with laundry tub

Boats with the laundry basket. As a boat, take the laundry basket and use the cardboard and broomstick as the paddles and ship off! When traveling by this boat, your kids will have more fun.

Balloon tennis with the paper plate

Tennis balloon with a paper cover. Paper sheets, plastic rulers, colored paper tape are all you need to DIY this tennis sheet of paper. Then enjoy this game of balloon tennis with your friends. Lots of fun to get quickly and easily, and the balloons are much easier to use than balls indoors.

Create New Fruit Snacks

Make Popsicles in Fresh Fruit. There is nothing better to beat the smoldering heat on a hot summer day than a cold Popsicle. So let your older children try their hand to make pops of this fresh fruit. It'll be meaningful, and they will appreciate it the most.

There is nothing better to beat the smoldering heat on a humid summer day than a cold Popsicle. So let your older children try their hand to make pops of this fresh fruit. It'll be meaningful, and they will appreciate it the most.

DIY Marble Run from Rolls Toilets

Toilet Rolls, DIY Marble Fly. If your kids love marble runs, finding a DIY marble run version that your kids might make is perfect.

Have an indoor camp-out?

Camping indoors is a fun activity for children while being healthier. Your kids should have fun planning out their campfire and enjoy spending the night in their own tent.

Camping indoors is a fun activity for children while being healthier. Your children should have fun planning out their "campfire" and enjoy spending the night in their own tent.

Flee the Volcano

This educational game will teach children about the identification of color, names of form, counting, and more.

Play with the wall of noodles

There are lots of fun with noodles in the water. This wall of water is no exception. Children are so happy about getting wet in the water, particularly during the summertime.

There are kinds of strange noodles with tub. This wall of water is no exception. Children are so happy about getting wet in the water, particularly during the summertime.

Build Rainbow Village

To make this rainbow village, use your free colorful card-stocks. Hold the houses together using bits of Velcro. Your children will create and recreate the rainbow village with various variations of colors over and over again.

Color Walk Playing

Game with Walk in Light. Get your kids off the sofa and work out with this game of jumping. Have a stack of paper lay down in a path through the house, with different colors. Keep separate colors. Children will have fun exploring various jumping styles.

Get your kids off the sofa and work out with this game of jumping. Have a stack of paper lay down in a path through the house, with different colors. Keep separate colors. Children will have fun exploring various jumping styles. Say, should she just make it from one end of the house to the other by walking on some colors?

Spay Exercise Game

Prepare other basic household things such as yarns or colored masking tapes and put them in your house well. Children will find it a big challenge to see who can pass through the lasers without touching them.

Prepare other basic household things such as yarns or colored masking tapes and put them in your house well. Children will consider it a huge challenge to see who can move through the "lasers" without hitting them.

Activity storytelling

Telling the tale of the action. This visual storytelling activity with painted stones will encourage the creativity of children and promote creative thinking. The combination of different characters can produce various interesting stories.

This visual storytelling activity with painted stones will encourage the creativity of children and promote creative thinking. The combination of different characters can produce various interesting stories.

Races powered by balloons

Children enjoy balloons forever. Round up some balloons, cords and LEGOs build the balloon-powered race game. This project may require a bit more work, but the end result for your little ones is a day full of happy memories.

Children enjoy balloons forever. Round up some balloons, strings, and LEGOs to build the balloon-powered race game. This project might take a little more effort, but the end result for your little ones is a day full of happy memories.

3.4 Indoor Fun Activities in winters

Yet every winter comes a time when no amount of bundling up will prevent the frigid cold from sending us back indoors. I'm thankful for the quieter months when we're reading endless books, playing fireside games, painting, and drawing, and just slowing down generally. Of course, when the dreaded winter crazies set in, there comes a time. The boys are becoming restless, chasing one another in circles, screaming about the house. They rough-house and bicker. And that's when I break out the Indoor Ideas list.

1. Build a house for playing cardboard (or rocket ship, or play dome)

Take from a nearby builder, furniture store, or another wholesale distribution warehouse a huge refrigerator box (often they're happy to give away big boxes). Tape one end shut and cover the sides with duct tape, then help your child cut a window and a door. Encourage your child to install control panels using items you have around your homes, such as string, bottle caps, and rolls of toilet paper or other recyclables.

2. Create dough for homemade play

This recipe smells way better than the store-bought stuff, plus it's going to make your kids so much fun, then play with it after it cools off.

3. Sumo Wrestling

When the children need to burn some steam indoors, clear out a living room space and line the corners with pillows. Let your kids borrow your old t-shirt, cover it with front and back pillows, and let them play with each other. Go ahead, try holding back your own laughter while you are refereeing the game.

4. Make marshmallow frames

Build something your child can imagine using dried spaghetti and mini marshmallows! Experiment with the power of different shapes and configurations, or take this opportunity to expose your little ones to geometry.

5. Make monster feet in the carton

Build a pair of monster feet that clip onto your child's feet with shoelaces with the leftover cardboard you have from the playroom.

6. Let your child take a bath in "Mad Scientist."

Gather plastic cups of different sizes, small containers, spray bottles and funnels, and set up a plastic stool in the water. Let your kid take a bath in the middle of the day without the intention of getting clean; instead, let him or her use the stool as a table to line up the "experiments." Add soap and bubbles and see what it comes up with.

7. Create a race route in marble

To make two racetracks, cut one pool noodle in half lengthwise using a serrated knife. Then put them on your stairs side-by-side or stand up against the sofa. Let the children race their marbles or tiny cars.

8. Scavenger hunt indoors

Hide hunting clues around the house, which will keep them occupied, solving riddles, and working as a team. Leave a "treasure box" for an extra special surprise at the end, with a few treats.

9. Build a table with tapestry

At a second-hand store, pick up an old coffee table frame and stitch a large piece of burlap around the rims. Using yarn and string scraps and sewing needles for big plastic dolls, and let your child learn how to sew on the tapestry table. It's perfect for their fine motor skills, and they can hang it up on the wall in their room when they're done.

10. Make a Lese Nook

You can turn to books forever! Check out your local library's giant bag of books, and when you return home, build a reading nook with pillows, blankets, and beloved stuffed animals in the cosiest spot in the building. Then join in with your child for a marathon reading.

Chapter 4: Fun Family Games for any Occasions

Friendly Games for Friends

There are plenty of enjoyable family games that can be integrated into bigger-scale activities like family reunions or children's birthday parties. Next time you've got a bigger group to share in the fun, check out the following ideas.

Classes

Categories make a play that's perfect for any size group, easy, educational, and fun. The game name says it all: one person comes up with a category, and each person after that has to say something that fits into that category without taking too much time. This game works best when it is played in a circle and at a particular beat. If the category, for example, is "animals," then within the allotted time, everyone has to name an animal such as "zebra" or "lion," or else they're out for the following rounds.

Duck, goose.

For a reason, this classic has stuck around through the years. Simple and active game: Perfect for children's groups. The person is chosen as "it" will go around the circle and tap each person saying "duck." When taping someone and saying "goose," the person will then chase the "it" around the circle and try marking them. If "it" is not tagged and the tagged person makes it into the spot left open, then it is "it."

Another classic, chairs, and a talker with music are the only materials you need for this game. Provide enough chairs in each round minus one for each, play the music and make each walk to the beat around the chairs circle. Everybody has to sit up in a chair when the music ends. Everyone who doesn't get a chair is out of the rounds below.

Fun Outdoor Games for family

Day

This classic outdoor game represents a perfect way to enjoy outdoor space. And to add a fun twist: consider wearing a custom cape to give "it" to make them feel extra fast.

Hide & Seek

Hide and seek can be played outdoors or indoors, but playing outside helps provide some fresh air for the entire family. Only make sure you set limits before the game begins.

Head & Jump in Balloon

This game seems easy, but it can be pretty hard to keep tuned! Fill a balloon (not helium) with air, so it will sink easily to the ground. Every player then try to keep it in the air by only head-butting it.

Simple and fun Games for a family reunion

Minnows and Sharks

Sharks and minnows start easy, with only one "shark" attempting to tag the "minnows" as they run across the designated play area. They become shark when a minnow is tagged too. The game ends when there's just one minnow left.

Calling

The telephone reveals how easy it can be to miscommunicate. Sit in a circle with the whole party, and ask one person to whisper a sentence into someone's ear. That message is then passed along with whispers and revealed when the person who started it reaches. Usually, those games end with some serious stupid sentences.

Who Am I?

Who Am I? Makes a perfect ice breaker for any reason, especially when you play with your family. It is especially fun. Place sticky notes on the front of each player with a character or human, and make each player's trying to guess who they are by asking questions about their different characteristics.

Two Realities and one lie

Another ice breaker, Party game turned: Two truths and a lie make the ultimate test for the best storytellers in the group. You just have to call two truths and one lie and try to guess what each other's lie is.

Games for the family to play at home

Whether the weather is bad or you are looking for some fun Christmas games during the winter months, staying indoors sometimes makes for a perfect venue for the game. Check out the following Family games fun ideas at home:

Illustration

A classic game for both good and bad artists, this game requires just a whiteboard or a paper stable, markers, a timer, and imagination.

Charades & Charades

Charades allow for a fun and engaging family activity for those who would rather act out scenes rather than the sketch. Draw the guys, positions, or stuff out of a hat and hold time for the guessing squad.

Minute for Victory

There is plenty of fun and competitive minute available to win it games, and these fast-paced games are perfect for a competitive night out.

Classic Fun Board Games

Jigsaw

Puzzles are perfect for a quiet night out in. They also help teach kids how to solve problems and how to work together.

Consider personalized puzzle sets to make your puzzle night even more special.

Monopolies

This classic board game evokes the competitive essence of the entire family. Only make sure everyone is ready for the game to last hours before anyone wins.

Candy Country

Candy soil is sweet and pleasant and suitable for any generation. Using simple game pieces and instructions, it doesn't usually last long, and then you'll have plenty of time to dessert.

Scrubbing

Not only has Scrabble stood the test of time (Words with Friends, anybody?) but still makes a relevant and educational game for the entire family. It can help teach children new words or strengthen more difficult ones, and reward those with great vocabulary or a lot of creativity.

4.1 Crazy Fun Family Games to Play Anywhere

1. Word Square-Show off with this fun game, your smarts, creativity, and skill! How many words can build yours without being blocked!? Supplies include a pencil and paper.

2. The Sentence Game-It's such a fun family game to play with a group of people. It's like a mix of Pictionary and camera – and the results are hilarious TODAY. To get exact instructions on how to play, click the link. There is also a prototype for the game which you can print on your computer. (Template is not needed, but it makes it easier.) Supplies: pencils and paper.

3. Classification – Categories has always been one of our favorite family games, it's like a handmade, classic favorite version. It keeps my children entertained, and we're always having fun thinking about using various 5-letter words and categories. Supplies: Paper and pencils. We also have a game of Spouse Categories, which is so fun!

4. Who Am I? – This is a game that everyone may have played at a party at least once, but it's also a family game that's quick and easy, last minute. To find out "who they are," every person gets 20 questions. When we play with our little kids, we like to use Disney characters and cartoons. Sometimes, only our extended family names can be included. Supplies: Paper and pencils.

5. The Name Game-This game is also known as the game where, for some reason, people are crying out loud!! Supplies: paper, pencil, and stopwatch.

6. Discretion-This family game is great for a large family dinner to watch. Supplies: Paper and pencils.

7. Take a hint – To play this fun and the tricky game, you will need two teams of 4 – give clues, but have only one chance to correctly guess the phrase. This is a game you want to watch out for! Supplies: Paper and pencils.

8. How Do You Doo – Close to naming the track, but you take turns to see how many songs you can guess for your team in 5 minutes just singing the word "doo." Supplies: pencil, paper, and stopwatch.

9. Film ID-This game is such fun! It's a bit like Catchphrase in that you're trying to get your team to guess what's on the card, but it's much more fun as you're vying against another team to see who can get their team to guess in the least amount of terms. Supplies: paper, pencil, and stopwatch.

10. Hang Man-This is a favorite family game. Most have been loaded with a hangman car trip! Make it more fun by adding rules like: you have to do a dumb job if you guess the wrong message. Supplies: Paper and pencils.

11. 4 Papers – Pick a category (such as movie titles or book titles), and each player must write down 3-4 items that suit the category on paper slips and place them in a pile. Divide into two teams. You are going to go through 4 rounds of play. Set

the timer for 1 minute for each round, and each player tries to get their team to guess as many paper clips as possible according to the ground rules. If your turn ends and the current slip hasn't been guessed yet, throw it back into the stack for someone else. Players are allowed one move per game. The paper goes back into the pile if they pass. Alternate between teams until all papers are done away with. Some players could go in twice. Add the score as you go, 1 point per slip, which has been correctly estimated. Put the papers in a pile again and start the next round. The team ends the day with the highest score wins lap 4! Round Rules: Round 1: Define the document without using any document terms. Sound effects allowed. No deeds. Round 2: You can only use one single word or sound effects. No deeds. Round 3: Fish. No sounds. Round 4: Frame Freeze. The team will close their eyes, and the player will take a single position/position and then tell the team to open their eyes. Players are unable to render or shift noises. Supplies: Paper and pencils.

12. Reverse Charades-Don't you like the spotlight when you're playing? This game is great as you behave as a group, and it's up to one person to guess the correct answer! Grab some slips of paper and get a few items written down for us to carry out. You determine the categories and how many points you need to qualify! If your co-worker thinks correctly before the timer runs out, you get the point! Gong is your family game night to be full of laughter. Supplies: Paper and pencils.

13. What If-Someone writes a scenario of "what if," then you pass it on to the next person. They fold it over and write the sentence "then." You read them out in a way that's very funny! Supplies: Paper and pencils.

14. who's telling the Truth-This is a very funny game; get to know your game/storytelling! We love family games which teach us about each other new things. Supplies: Paper and pencils.

15. Mafia-In this fun game, you can't trust anyone! Try to figure out who the mafia members are without knowing who you can trust-and before they kill you! Supplies: Paper and pencils. We have a Murder Mystery Party for a fun group date that's ONE fun!

16. Word Ladder – By modifying only one letter at a time, who can build the shortest ladder between two words? Supplies: Paper and pencils.

4.2 Games to Play at Parties

1. Post It Game

A sticky stack of notes and a pad will be necessary. Write a name on each note of a well-known public figure or character, then pass it around until everybody has one. Every person should be sticking their note on their foreheads or back without looking. Mingle anyone, or sit in a circle and turn to ask yes or no questions to discover your given identity. ("I'm living?" is a perfect starting point.) Play until everyone's done correctly guesses their name, or give out prizes to people who first guess correct.

2. Saran Wrap Spin

This one takes a little preparation: You'll need a plastic wrap box and a candy bag, or an array of small, sturdy treats. (Gum packs, dollar bills, lottery tickets and the like) Choose one item with your saran wrap ball in the center. Thoroughly wrap it in plastic wrap, then add additional items as your wrapped ball grow bigger, trapping them in wrap layers. (To make the game more difficult, rip the wrap into smaller sheets as you go.) You're ready to play after you've used a whole roll of wrap (or more, if desired).

Assemble around a table or in a circle. Give the wrapped bundle to one person; give a pair of dice to the person beside them. The person who has the saran wrap package must remove as much of the ball as possible before doubling the person with the dice rolls. (It is yours to keep any prizes that fall out during your turn.) If the person with the dice rolls doubles, they move the dice down and obtain a package. Repeat until the ball has completely unwound.

Let the person with the plastic wrap ball wear oven mitts for alternate models, or set one-timer for each turn instead of using dice.

3. What's yours like?

To be "It," choose one person and send them out of the room. Choose a common trait with the remaining people: hair, clothing items, or body parts all work. When the person comes back, they will ask somebody, "What's yours? "That person should then give an adjective of a single word to describe its trait. (For example, itchy, thick and stretchy all work for shirts.) Repeat until the person who asks guesses the trait.

4. I never have

Sit in a circle. Start with one person saying, "I never have ..." and finish with something they never did. (Travelled to Africa, ate escargot, and the like of all work.) If anyone has done it, they must hold one finger up; if no one in the community has done it, the person who says, "I never have ..." must hold his finger up. Continue around the circle until you have three fingers up one person: they're out. This game of party can get as racy as you do, so if grandparents or other conservative guests are involved, play carefully, and set ground rules ahead of time.

5. Most Wanted To

For small groups of friends or family members, this Party game works best. A rally into a circle. Start by asking one guy, "Who's most likely to fly over their own feet?" (Or another scenario, feature, behavior, etc.) Count down from three (you are encouraged to perform a drumroll with your hands) and then point out who they think is most likely to perform the act. Whoever has the most pointed fingers, is out. Go around the circle and ask, "Who's most likely to ..." until it's all but one out. To make the game last longer, you can skip the eliminations.

6. Will you please?

A rally into a circle. Ask the person next to you and include two challenging situations, "Would you rather ...." ("Wouldn't you rather rinse your teeth for a year or not brush your teeth for a year?" for instance.) It's their turn to ask the individual alongside them after their answer. Continue until there are no more possibilities you can think of.

7. Heads Over!

This game needs an App: The Heads Up! The app's available from the Google Play and App Store. After buying and downloading the 99 cents, though, you always have hours of entertainment on hand. (In-app purchases are also available.) One guy, facing out, will hold a telephone to his forehead. While the person with the phone guesses, everyone else must carry out or explain whatever appears on the screen. They have as many correct guesses as possible for one minute, and then the phone goes on to the next person. Categories include animals, movies, celebrities, and public figures, and more.

8. Chairs to music

Okay, it's a popular children's party game, but adults can get in on that fun too. Place chairs (or cushions for seats) in a circle, facing outwards, with enough seats for all to play, minus one. Designate the music player to one person, and make everyone else stand around the seating circle in a circle. Rolling around the seats when the music starts, everybody has to find a seat when the music ends. Whoever aren't out?

Remove one more chair and start over again, until two people fight for one seat.

To make musical chairs more fun, add your own rules. Enable people, for example, to sit upside down (as long as their feet are off the floor), or make your own alterations.

9. I host a band

Play this Brain-teaser for a more cognitive game. Say you're hosting a party, and an invitation is being given only to people who bring the right contributions. Pick a hidden rule: Usually, everyone must bring something that starts with the same letter as their name, but you can also get more creative about it. Don't mention their law to someone else.

Go around the room and tell every person what they are bringing with them; respond with a "Yes, you're invited," or "No, you can't bring that," to each suggestion. Continue until everyone figures out the rule.

10. Two Realities and one lie

For example, pick three statements to make about yourself: "I have two brothers, I have been to three continents, and I love cats." Two are to be true; one is to be a lie. Everybody else has to guess what the lie is and then the next person goes. This is a great game of getting-to-know-you; whether you're playing with family or friends, select obscure information to try to confuse one another to make it even more enjoyable.

11. Calling

An oldie but a goodie: Assemble in a circle. Choose one sentence to whisper in next to your person's ear — no repeats. That person will whisper to the person next to them what they've heard, and so on until the sentence gets back to you. Prepare to joke at how this gets twisted. Play music in the background to make this harder.

12. Stalker with sticker

Buy sticker package. (This one is a perfect game for Christmas party or Halloween party, so try to find out the right stickers.) Give each one a sheet of five to ten stickers (or less, depending on the party size). The game plays best in a group where everyone mingles, and you can easily integrate it into the feature of your happy hour or neighborhood. Each person must discreetly place all of their stickers on guests from other parties; the first person to use all of their stickers wins. When they are caught stickering others, they will accept a sticker. You might laugh at the end of the evening at how sly those people are — and wonder how you ended up with stickers all over your back without even knowing.

4.3 Birthday Party Games for Kids

1. Award Walk

This game is similar to a cakewalk and is ideal for children aged between 2 and 4.

How do Game Play

Write numbers from 1 to 30 in square charts and place them within a circle on the wall. Create the same number of smaller chits and line them up in a basket. Play some music and let the kids walk around the room. When the music stops, tell them to stand on a level. If they pick up their number from the basket, they will win a draw. For a set number of rounds, the game can continue.

2. Bubble Race Cover

This easy game is undeniably enjoyable and appropriate for children older than three years. What could be any better? It needs only a little space and a lot of bubble wrap.

How do Game Play

Roll out in an open space, a large sheet of bubble wrap to the table. Now tell the kids to cross the bubble wrap without any of the bubbles bursting through. The kid who wins the game, crossing without any noise.

3. Scavenger Hunt video

Cruiser Hunt

This game can be played in by children of all ages, and playable anywhere. The level of difficulty needs to be adjusted according to the age of the children. Young kids can have a basic version of the game, and older kids can have a slightly more complicated version of the game.

How do Game Play

Sketch a map for the kids, tell them where to go, and give them image hints of what they need to find. Keep chocolates or bonuses along with each of those hints. If this game is being played in a public room, make sure to send an adult to chaperone the children.

4. Balloon flares

This game is great for children over the age of 4, and will certainly make you laugh a lot.

How do Game Play

Write down several obstacles on chit's paper and insert them before inflating them into various balloons. For as long as there is music, the kids will have to bop the balloon in the air. Once the music ends, it has to pop up the person who was the last to reach the balloon and execute the challenge inside it. It could be anything like dancing, leaking their elbow, and so on. Get creative on the challenges you face.

5. Boat Race on Deck

This interesting game is ideal for children over five years of age and requires only a few paper boats and a water tub.

How do Game Play

Create paper boats, and hand one for each boy, along with a straw. Kids would need to use the straw to blow air into the boats and push them into a plastic tub. The first person to take the boat onto the other side successfully wins the game.

Conclusion

It helps to gain trust in oneself. "Taking part in games that deliver both a sense of challenge and a sense of obligation achievement helps develop self-esteem and self-efficacy for your child — a feeling I can! "Walter says.

It promotes skills that are essential. Players can engage in all kinds of valuable skills, including problem-solving and decision-making, impulse control (waiting for your turn), rules and instructions, and contact with others. "It also helps some children to learn how to deal with conflict (How do you feel and behave when you don't win?) And clarify their values (would you like to lend money to others in a game like Monopoly? Save money? Build as many properties as you can?)"

It offers lifelong memories. Gambling together is a fun way for parents and children to interact beyond the slog of homework, errands, and chores. "We will look back on those times in the future and say, 'Remember when we did this or that together and how funny it was? '"Gladding says. "It fosters a parent-child relationship that goes beyond this day, or this week, or even this year. It will last a lifetime.'